CREEPY CHRONICLES

Witches, Wizards, and Dark Magic

Written by Barbara Cox and Scott Forbes

 Gareth Stevens
Publishing

CONTENTS

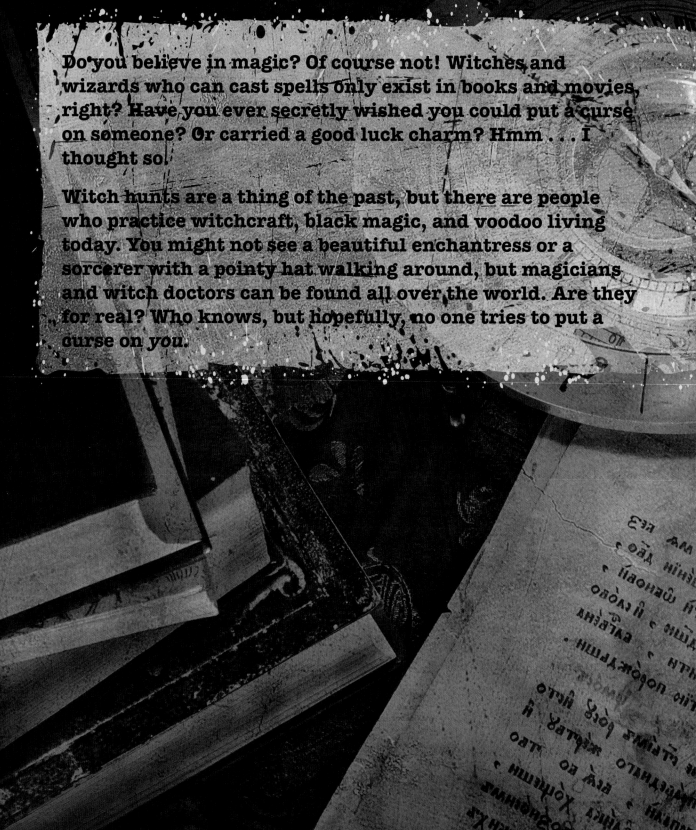

Do you believe in magic? Of course not! Witches and wizards who can cast spells only exist in books and movies, right? Have you ever secretly wished you could put a curse on someone? Or carried a good luck charm? Hmm . . . I thought so!

Witch hunts are a thing of the past, but there are people who practice witchcraft, black magic, and voodoo living today. You might not see a beautiful enchantress or a sorcerer with a pointy hat walking around, but magicians and witch doctors can be found all over the world. Are they for real? Who knows, but hopefully, no one tries to put a curse on *you*.

WITCHES, WIZARDS, AND DARK MAGIC

SPELLS AND HEXES

SPELLS are magical words that control people or things, such as turning them into another creature, making them act a certain way, or even killing them. Spells may not always be evil, and can sometimes be cast to make good things happen, like falling in love or getting well. However, hexes, jinxes, and curses are definitely not good.

GOOD AND BAD SPELLS

The most reliable sign that someone has magical ability—whether good or evil—is their ability to cast hexes and spells. If you can cast a spell on someone or something, you can make that person or thing do what you want. So, for instance, you can make somebody go cross-eyed, turn them into a rabbit, or you can cause normal food to suddenly give terrible indigestion to everybody who eats it.

If you have even more power, you can command the weather. More seriously still, you can make your enemies insane or die a terrible death. Only one exact combination of words, with perhaps the mixing of special ingredients to be burned or eaten, will achieve the required effect. Witches and wizards spend their lives learning these formulas, acquiring spells of increasing power as they get older, until they're practically ancient and know some extremely dangerous spells.

For those of us who are not witches or wizards, the best thing is to know something about spells, so that we have some idea what to do if we should ever find ourselves under a spell for whatever reason.

INCANTATIONS

An incantation is the words of a spell, which usually must be said aloud a set number of times for the spell to take effect.

The moon is often important when casting spells. A spell cast at full moon will be more powerful. A spell to get rid of something or someone will work better when the moon is "waning" (fading), while a spell to summon something or someone will be more suited to the "waxing" (growing) moon.

Symbols are frequently used in spells, whether they're drawn on the floor or on a piece of paper that might be burned as the spell is cast. Typical symbols used are the pentagram, hexagram, and spiral.

POTIONS

Potions are spells that are magically contained in drinks. They can have strong or lesser effects. If taken by accident, they are usually difficult to counteract and have to be allowed to wear off.

HEXES AND JINXES

A hex is usually a spell of general misfortune. The word comes from the German *hexe*, meaning "witch." If someone has a hex put on them, from that moment on nothing will go right in their lives.

A jinx is like a hex, but not as bad, often causing someone to fail in a sport or at work. Many people believe that, even without knowledge of magic, you can accidentally put a jinx on a sports player or team if you talk over-confidently about how well they'll play.

WITCH

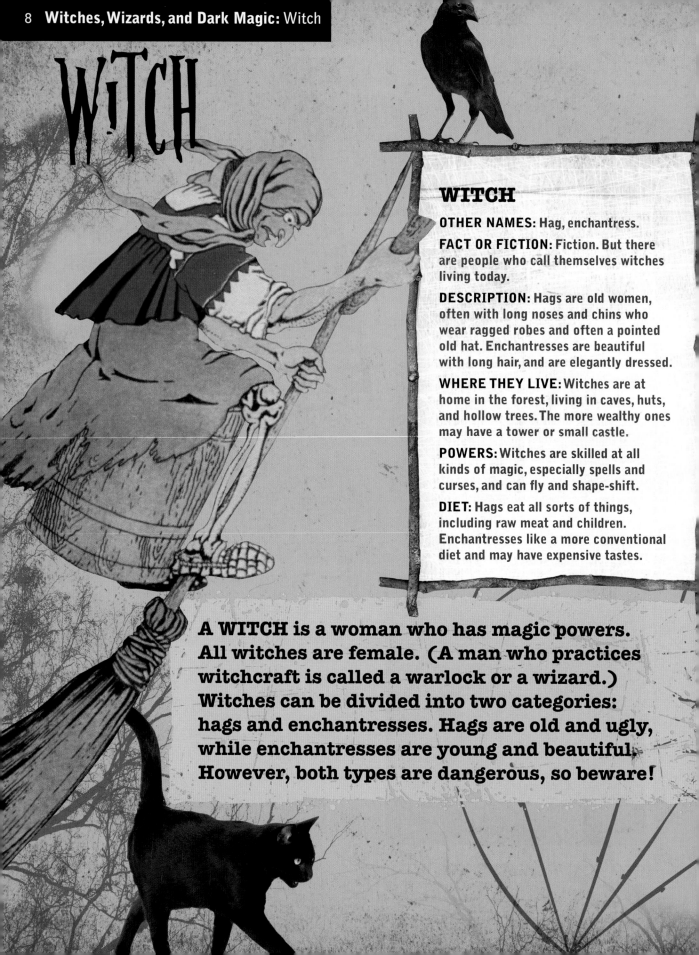

WITCH

OTHER NAMES: Hag, enchantress.

FACT OR FICTION: Fiction. But there are people who call themselves witches living today.

DESCRIPTION: Hags are old women, often with long noses and chins who wear ragged robes and often a pointed old hat. Enchantresses are beautiful with long hair, and are elegantly dressed.

WHERE THEY LIVE: Witches are at home in the forest, living in caves, huts, and hollow trees. The more wealthy ones may have a tower or small castle.

POWERS: Witches are skilled at all kinds of magic, especially spells and curses, and can fly and shape-shift.

DIET: Hags eat all sorts of things, including raw meat and children. Enchantresses like a more conventional diet and may have expensive tastes.

A **WITCH** is a woman who has magic powers. All witches are female. (A man who practices witchcraft is called a warlock or a wizard.) Witches can be divided into two categories: hags and enchantresses. Hags are old and ugly, while enchantresses are young and beautiful. However, both types are dangerous, so beware!

BE WITCHED!

Witches are famous for casting spells. They have a great store of magic knowledge, which they can use to do anything from summoning up the spirits of the dead to turning naughty little boys into toads. Not all of their magic is harmful—they're quite capable of healing and doing good, but they have plenty of magic weapons at their command if anyone should annoy them. Enchantresses can become very fond of human men and will cast some unpleasant curses if they're rejected by them.

Almost all witches can shape-shift (turn themselves into something else) if they want to. They may prowl through the forest in the form of a large wildcat or a she-wolf, or fly through the night skies as a bird of prey. Witches can also learn things about distant or future events by gazing into a mirror or a crystal ball (this is called "scrying")—though other people can do this too and not all fortune-tellers are witches!

WITCHES' SABBATH

The Witches' Sabbath is the name given to the nocturnal meetings of a group of witches, where they get into all sorts of evil things! Although called the Sabbath, it can take place on any day of the week.

BUBBLE BUBBLE TOIL AND TROUBLE

Witches' spells are often made in the form of a "potion," or magic drink—one that may seem quite normal and even delicious, but a few sips of which can have an unexpected effect, turning the drinker into a donkey, stone, centipede, or anything else the witch's warped sense of humor has devised. For this reason it is very unwise either to upset a witch or, if you should happen to find one at home, to have a drink with her. Traditionally the potions are brewed in a huge, round metal pot called a cauldron.

GRIMOIRES

A grimoire is a witches' handbook. Inside it is all kinds of information, from details about how a witch should dress, what tools to use and how to make them and, of course, spells. There are charms, incantations, and rituals to follow. There are some actual grimoires still in existence from the Middle Ages, from people who called themselves sorcerers.

FLY WITCH FLY

All witches can fly. They use a variety of things to fly in or on, from a forked wand or spade to an airborne bicycle. In ancient Greece and Rome, the power of flight was always associated with witchcraft. Witches would either transform themselves into birds to fly, or they might fly on the backs of animals. But by far the most popular flying aid is a broomstick. It must be an old-fashioned broom known as a besom, which has a bundle of twigs tied to a wooden handle. Riding this, a witch can fly far and fast, making her extremely hard to catch and therefore safe from enemies. Witches will fly long distances to attend meetings with other witches, called "covens."

WICCA

Not all witchcraft is evil. In recent times a certain type of "magic" has become popular again, called Wicca. (The word is taken from the Old English word for "wise.") This kind of witchcraft is considered helpful, and its followers believe that they can solve problems and cure diseases using various spells and potions that are based on ancient traditions. There are even shops in major cities that sell the ingredients needed— from dragon's blood powder and devil's shoestring, to mixes that are said to attract love or money or create a peaceful home.

WITCH DOCTORS

A witch doctor is a very different thing from a witch. A witch doctor is someone living in tribal cultures of Africa, Central America, and the Caribbean, who practices magic as part of the tribe's religion. The term "witch doctor" is very old-fashioned, and today we would call these people medicine men or shamen.

These medicine men use their magical powers for healing, telling the future, and protecting the tribe from, or getting rid of, evil spirits.

MORGAN LE FAY

Morgan le Fay, or Morgana, might look beautiful but don't be fooled —she was a nasty piece of work and caused her half-brother, King Arthur of Camelot, endless problems. In some stories, Morgan was an evil fairy ("le Fay" means "the fairy"), while others have it that she was just a wicked human with magical powers, specializing in the black arts that some say she learned from the great wizard Merlin.

Always on the lookout for a handsome knight to bewitch, Morgan took a particular liking to Sir Lancelot, who unfortunately was already in love with Queen Guinevere. Although she was her lady in waiting, Morgan was jealous of Guinevere and began to hate her with a passion. She decided to tell King Arthur about Guinevere and Lancelot.

She made a magical horn from which only "honest" women could drink, in order to expose the cheating Guinevere. Morgan also stole Arthur's famous sword, Excalibur, and sent it to Arthur's enemy in a desperate attempt to overthrow him.

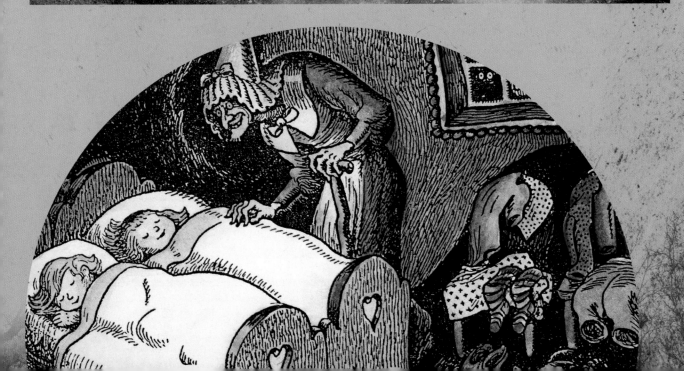

THE FAMILIAR

Every witch has a Familiar. This is a spirit that takes the form of an animal— usually a black cat; a bird such as a crow, owl, or magpie; or sometimes even a toad, rat, mouse, squirrel, or spider. The Familiar is the witch's companion, but it's much more than a pet. As a powerful spirit, it helps the witch to perform magic spells and rites, and protects her against enemies. Sometimes the Familiar is more magically powerful than the witch herself. Familiars often have strange names. Some famous Familiars of fiction have been called Pyewacket, Vinegar Tom, and Grizzel Greediguts.

For centuries, people were suspicious of any black cat in case it was a witch's Familiar, but in fact there was no need to worry about this, since most black cats have absolutely no magical ability whatsoever. If you ever meet a black cat that genuinely is a witch's Familiar, you'll know because your hair will stand on end and you'll feel very uncomfortable.

A few centuries ago, witch-hunters would often need no more proof that a woman was a witch than the fact that she lived alone and owned a pet cat, bird, or mouse!

QUEEN ANNE BOLEYN

Anne Boleyn, second wife of King Henry VIII of England from 1533–36, was believed by some people to be a witch because she had six fingers on one hand and a lump on her neck. These were thought to be typical signs that a woman was a witch. The gossip was that she had taken the king away from his first wife by casting spells on him. This was really all part of a plot to enable Henry to get rid of her and marry someone else.

Below: Not all witches were ugly old hags who lived in hovels. There were thought to be witches among the rich and powerful, too.

WITCHES' HATS

Witches supposedly wear tall, black, pointed hats. However, very old stories and legends about witches don't usually mention witches wearing hats. During the time of the Salem witch trials in seventeenth-century America, tall pointed hats happened to be the fashion of the time, so that might be why witches have been shown wearing hats like that ever since.

BABA YAGA

Baba Yaga was an old and ugly Russian witch who liked to eat people (especially children). She flew around in a huge magic mortar, steering it with the pestle and sweeping up the wind with her witch's broom to help her fly faster. Baba Yaga was best known for her house, which could be found deep in the forest. It stood on chicken legs and feet. The house could run through the trees screeching horribly, but it would come back to its permanent place in a yard closed in by a fence of bones with skulls along the top.

TESTS TO IDENTIFY A WITCH

For a long time, roughly between the fifteenth and eighteenth centuries, people throughout Europe (and later North America) believed that witches were living amongst them and were plotting to destroy Christianity. Many ordinary women (and some men) were accused of being witches and were forced to go through tests to prove their innocence.

They would be:

- Examined for marks on their bodies
- Deprived of sleep
- Tortured to make them confess, using the rack or thumbscrew
- Burned, since it was believed that a witch could not heal from a burn
- Dunked in water because it was believed that a witch would always float. If they were proved to be witches they would be burned at the stake.

WITCH HUNTS

At different times in history, people have become afraid of the power of witches and have tried to hunt them all down and destroy them. This unfortunately led to people who were not witches being accused of witchcraft and often unfairly tortured and even killed.

From medieval times until the seventeenth century, certain men took it upon themselves to become official witch hunters. In 1644 a man in England named Matthew Hopkins supposedly discovered his first six witches in Essex. After this he was named Witch Finder General, and he proceeded to cause havoc, accusing women all over the place of practicing witchcraft. Generally he would force a confession from the innocent women and then they would be hanged.

In 1692 in the small town of Salem, Massachusetts, two young girls began to behave strangely and a number of adults were accused of bewitching them. Soon almost everyone in the town was accusing each other of witchcraft, and a series of trials took place. Twenty-three people were found guilty and imprisoned or even executed. Either there was a freakishly high population of witches in Salem or someone made a very big mistake and many innocent people lost their lives.

CIRCE

Circe was a mythical Greek enchantress who lived in a forest. She was very beautiful, but could be cruel and vengeful, especially to men who rejected her. She was an expert poisoner and was famous for turning anyone who annoyed her into an animal or bird. The most famous story about Circe tells of a band of Greeks led by Odysseus on their long journey to get home after the Trojan War. They arrived at Circe's palace, and she entertained them, but the men annoyed her and she gave them a potion that turned them into pigs. Only Odysseus was still in human shape since the god Hermes had given him a special herb to protect him. He pleaded with Circe to transform the pig-men back, and in the end she agreed, but only if they stayed with her for a year and a day.

WIZARD

OTHER NAMES: Magician, sorcerer, warlock, enchanter, magus, alchemist, shaman.

FACT OR FICTION: Fiction, though many people throughout history have claimed to be wizards.

DESCRIPTION: Usually, wizards are men with long white hair and beards. They wear robes, a cape (often covered with stars or magical symbols) and a pointed hat, and carry a staff or magic wand.

WHERE THEY LIVE: Richer wizards inhabit castles and towers, though some of these may be old ruins. Others live in caves and forest hollows.

POWERS: Wizards can create magic potions, cast spells, hypnotize people, see into and influence the future, and change themselves and other people into animals.

WEAKNESSES: Often old, so they tend to be a little slow moving. But don't let appearances deceive—their magic works fast and is powerful!

OTHER CHARACTERISTICS: Interested in the magical properties of numbers and astrology.

FAMOUS WIZARDS: Merlin, Dr. John Dee, Nicolas Flamel, Nostradamus, Gandalf, Dumbledore, Harry Potter.

WIZARD

WIZARDS, who are usually men, use magic and spells to make things happen. Many are good and employ their powers to help others, but some, especially those known as sorcerers, prefer to taunt, terrify, and torment. Good magic is known as "white magic," whereas magic used for evil purposes is "black magic."

CASTING A SPELL

Wizards call up supernatural spirits and forces and make them work on their behalf. They do this by casting spells. Casting a spell might involve chanting a series of phrases while making certain gestures, or giving someone a potion to drink.

Before performing a spell, a wizard may draw a circle on the ground with chalk or salt, known as a magic circle. He may place the items required for the spell inside this circle to concentrate its power, or he may stand inside it when pronouncing the spell to protect himself from the dangerous forces he is unleashing.

CONTROLLING NATURE

Wizards have power over the elements—air, earth, fire, and water. They can provoke storms, floods, fires, and earthquakes.

Some can call upon evil demons to do their dirty work, including mandragoras, tiny servants of the devil. Others can turn into other creatures at will—and even fly.

WIZARD WAYS

In some societies, wizards are important figures. But in others they are outcasts, often feared and despised, who live alone in remote towers and have to be sought out by people who need their help. Wizards learn their magic from older wizards. They compile libraries of books of spells and store jars full of magical plants and other substances for making potions. Every wizard needs a staff or wand to channel and direct his magic. It is usually made of wood and sometimes decorated with magical symbols. Without it, spells may be less effective or not work at all.

ANIMAL COMPANIONS

Like witches, wizards also have companions, known as Familiars. These are supernatural spirits that assume the form of animals—most often cats, toads, owls, and rats—to help protect the wizard.

Below: Merlin and King Arthur find the sword, Excalibur.

MERLIN

Apart from Harry Potter, probably the most famous wizard of all is Merlin, who appears in the old English legends of King Arthur. The character was based on a sixth-century Welsh hermit called Myrddin. In some of the legends, Merlin is a sinister sorcerer, renowned for his shape-shifting. However, in others he is King Arthur's kindly adviser and protector. When he was very old, Merlin decided to share his wizard secrets with the woman Niviane, whom he loved. However, she was deceitful and used Merlin's powers against him to trap him in a tomb forever.

SECOND SIGHT

Any decent wizard should be able to predict the future—a practice known as divination or scrying. To do this, he might rely on second sight, which are visions simply popping into his head, or he might peer into a crystal ball (a common wizard tool) and see future events unfolding there.

The early sixteenth-century French wizard Michel de Nostradame, also known as Nostradamus, had his own particular technique. He would fill a bowl with water and place it on a brass tripod. After touching his wand to the tripod, the water, and his robe, he would stare into the water, waiting for images of the future to appear. He wrote them all down as verses. After some seemed to come true, he was invited to work at the court of the king, Henri II of France.

THE PHILOSOPHER'S STONE

In the Middle Ages, many wizards became obsessed with discovering a method for turning common metals into gold, a practice known as alchemy. In turn, they thought this would give them the power to cure all illness and let people live forever. The key to making all this happen was thought to be a substance called the Philosopher's Stone. Searching for the stone, wizards pored over ancient books, ground up minerals, boiled chemicals, and whipped up potions.

Frenchman Nicolas Flamel claimed to have found the Philosopher's Stone in the early 1400s. No evidence to support his claim has been found—though he did die a very wealthy man.

BLACK MAGIC

BLACK MAGIC is generally unfriendly magic, and involves enchantments in connection with death, damage, and destruction. Obviously only evil witches and wizards use this type of magic.

NASTY STUFF

Black magic is dangerous stuff and should be avoided by anyone with good sense. It often involves using the spirits or bodies of the dead to harm the living. It can be used to bring illness, bad luck, unhappiness, madness, or death to someone who is the enemy of the magician.

Like most magic, it cuts both ways: you can't cast a powerful black magic spell without also harming yourself. Those who use black magic can persuade themselves that they're strong enough to handle it, but they will almost certainly be wrong. A powerful magician may be able to summon up a demon to carry out a murderous errand for him, but the price to be paid may be very high—his soul, for example.

TYPES OF MAGIC

Magic spells and rituals are categorized according to the purpose for which they are used:

- Black magic is for damage, destruction, and death.
- White magic is for healing and good luck.
- Green magic is used to make things grow and to attract money.
- Red magic is for love and passion.
- Purple magic is for gaining power.

TUPILAK

A TUPILAK is a kind of "devil doll" that is used in traditional Inuit culture to bring harm to an enemy. Inuit magicians would make a carved doll to carry all their curses and bad wishes to their enemies. It was believed that an evil spirit would take possession of the doll.

DEVIL DOLL

The Inuits are the native peoples of the Arctic region of North America and Europe.

Inuit magicians would make a Tupilak doll at night, in absolute secrecy, creating it out of parts of animals. They would add more spells in stages over several nights until it was powerful enough to do all kinds of bad things. It was believed that, in many cases, when the Tupilak was finished, an evil spirit would actually have taken possession of it. Again in secret, the magician would put the possessed doll into the sea with special magic instructions so that it would float to where the enemy was living and bring evil to that person.

However, there was a catch. If the enemy was also strong in magic, they could reverse the Tupilak and send it back, and it would do all the bad things to the magician who had sent it, and their village too. The only way out was for the magician to confess to having made the doll, which would then lose its power.

Below: An eighteenth-century Voodoo ritual of human sacrifice.
Opposite page, top left: African Voodoo fetish.

VOODOO

VOODOO is an African-Caribbean religion with a reputation for using spells and curses. Black Voodoo magic, such as Zombies and Voodoo dolls, have become well known through stories in books and movies—so much so that many people think that's all there is to Voodoo. However, Voodoo is a religion that has both its good and scary sides, but we are looking at the scary side in this book!

LEFT- AND RIGHT-HAND MAGIC

Voodoo has its own witches and wizards. Healing and helpful voodoo magic is called "magic of the right hand," while black or evil Voodoo magic is called "magic of the left hand." Most Voodoo magicians will only do one kind, though a few will work "with both hands."

VOODOO DOLL

Another famous aspect of Voodoo black magic is the use of dolls. A Voodoo doll or gris-gris can be made to represent your enemy, and you can then stick pins in it, with appropriate spells and curses, to make the enemy suffer.

In fact, you can make a doll for good purposes as well, and can even make a gris-gris of yourself and stick the right kind of pins in to bring yourself good luck—but the bad kind is more frequently used.

The dolls are traditionally made out of sticks bound together with moss and then wrapped in strips of fabric. A face can be stitched onto the fabric.

It may not be necessary even to stick pins in the doll. Marie Laveau, a famous Voodoo magician from New Orleans, used to leave a gris-gris doll on the doorstep of people she wanted to influence. They would be terrified that a hex had been put on them and would come to Marie for guidance on how to get rid of this curse. She would then be able to persuade them to pay her money, or do whatever else she wanted them to do, so that the supposed hex could be lifted.

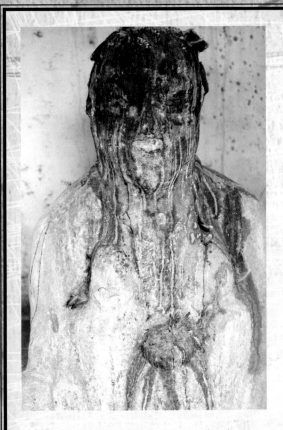

THE VOODOO RELIGION

Voodoo, or vodoun, is a religion descended from a mixture of African beliefs and Roman Catholic Christianity. It began in the days of slavery, but is still practiced today, most commonly in Haiti and in Louisiana. In Voodoo, it is believed that there is one supreme God, but everyday affairs are ruled by the Loa, who are powerful spirits with different areas of responsibility.

ZOMBIE

One very famous part of Voodoo black magic is the use of Zombies. These are dead people who are under a spell that makes them walk around and do whatever the magician commands.

Right: The wicked fairy from "Sleeping Beauty" putting an enchantment on the sleeping baby princess.

POSSESSION

A person or thing is taken over by an unseen force.

A person is said to be "possessed" when it seems that an evil force has taken over their body and is making them do and say bad things against their will. Animals and even objects can also be possessed. There have been numerous well-known cases of possessed people throughout history. However, it's important to remember that, in modern times, many of these supposed "possessions" would now be diagnosed as mental illnesses or conditions such as epilepsy.

EXORCISM

A religious ceremony to rid a place or person of evil influences.

Sometimes a place is being used by a spirit or poltergeist to such an extent that people find it impossible to live there, and something has to be done to make the spirit move on. Most major religions have an established ceremony for exorcism, including prayers and ritual gestures such as sprinkling holy water. A priest will try to communicate with the unwanted spirit, and either persuade it to leave or threaten it with punishment from higher beings if it doesn't go. This usually works. Exorcism can also be tried when a person is believed to be possessed, though good results are less predictable.

ENCHANTMENT

ENCHANTMENTS are strong spells. They are not considered black magic, but they can have dangerous consequences. Enchantments are cast by powerful magicians and enchanters.

FAMOUS ENCHANTMENTS

Many famous fairy tales contain enchantments. In "Sleeping Beauty," the princess is magically plunged into deep sleep for 100 years until a prince fights his way through the forest and breaks the spell. In "Beauty and the Beast," a prince is enchanted and has to live as a monster until someone loves him the way he is, as a monster. This kind of long-term enchantment can be seen as an imprisoning spell—the person is not killed or permanently harmed, but is locked in a magical state until someone else releases them. Often the conditions for ending the enchantment are very difficult, so the chances of rescue are slim. In Hans Christian Andersen's "The Wild Swans," Elisa's brothers are turned into swans and can only be turned back if she makes shirts for all of them out of stinging nettles. She must also not speak a word, or they will die. Only remarkable courage or selflessness will break this kind of spell.

Left: An eighteenth-century priest carries out an exorcism.

AMULETS AND TALISMANS

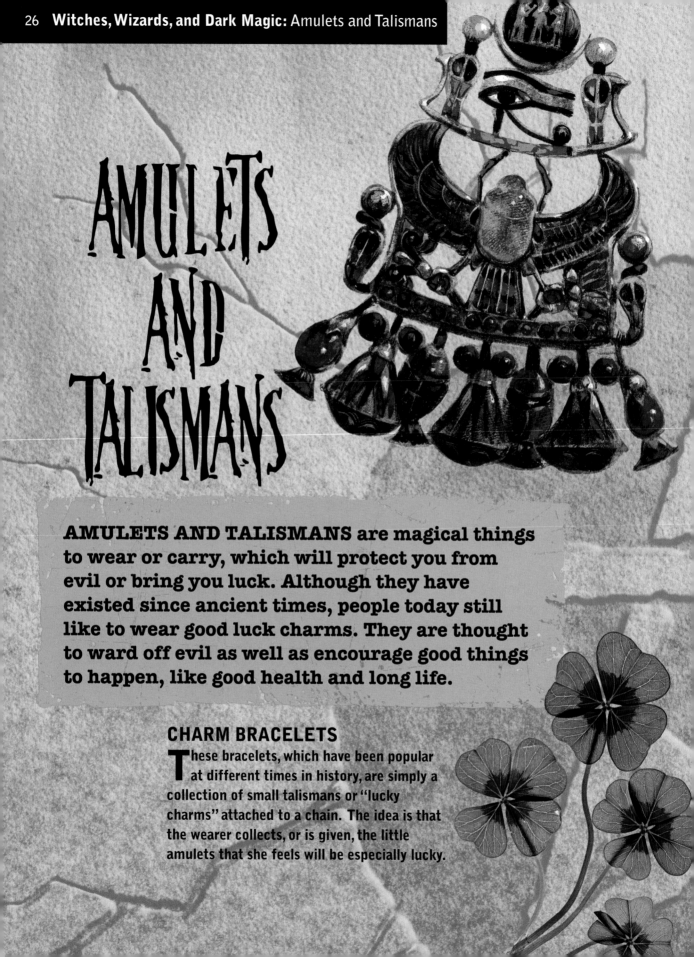

AMULETS AND TALISMANS are magical things to wear or carry, which will protect you from evil or bring you luck. Although they have existed since ancient times, people today still like to wear good luck charms. They are thought to ward off evil as well as encourage good things to happen, like good health and long life.

CHARM BRACELETS

These bracelets, which have been popular at different times in history, are simply a collection of small talismans or "lucky charms" attached to a chain. The idea is that the wearer collects, or is given, the little amulets that she feels will be especially lucky.

PROTECTION

The wearing of amulets and talismans has a very long history. In ancient Egypt, most of the jewelry that people wore had a special meaning. Most pieces were for protection against bad luck or to bring good things into the wearer's life. A frequently used talisman was the scarab beetle or "khepera," which was associated with the creator god Atum and with the sun. Egyptians were often buried with a khepera amulet over their heart; it was supposed to give protection when their soul would be weighed by the gods to see if it was worthy to enter the afterlife.

In ancient Rome, each child was given a protective amulet, which he or she wore all the time until they grew up. Boys would wear an amulet called a "bulla," while girls wore a moon-shaped pendant called a "lunula."

Traditional amulets in Middle Eastern and Asian countries include the "hamsa," or hand, to protect against evil influences, and the fish which brings fertility and prosperity. Chinese culture has a long tradition of wearing amulets engraved with various symbols such as "double happiness" or the dragon for courage.

MODERN AMULETS AND TALISMANS

In the modern world, many of us still wear or use talismans and amulets, without calling them by those names. People will choose a piece of jewelry connected with their sign of the zodiac, because they believe it will be lucky for them. Many people like to wear the "birthstone" that's considered lucky for people with their birth month—for example, topaz for those born in November. We often also pick our lucky color or number.

A bride is supposed to wear "something old, something new, something borrowed, and something blue" to bring her luck on her wedding day and afterward in her marriage. There are many people who go to an exam or a job interview carrying or wearing something they believe is lucky, whether it's a special coin, stone, a handkerchief embroidered with a four-leaf clover, or even a rabbit's foot. We still think of horseshoes as lucky, too.

Top left: Amulet found in the tomb of Egyptian pharaoh King Tutankhamun.
Top right: A pentagram pendant.
Right: Egyptian gold scarab.

GLOSSARY

Alchemy: a medieval chemical science with the goals of changing less valuable metals into gold

Ancient: of or relating to a period of time long past

Astrology: the study of the supposed influences of the stars on human affairs by their positions in relation to each other

Cauldron: a large kettle

Coven: a meeting or band of witches

Divination: the art or practice of using omens or magic powers to foretell the future

Epilepsy: a disorder marked by abnormal electrical discharges in the brain, by attacks of convulsions, and by loss of consciousness

Hex: a spell of general misfortune

Hovel: an open shed or shelter

Incantation: a series of words used to produce a magic spell

Jinx: someone or something that brings bad luck

Legend: a story coming down from the past whose truth is popularly accepted but cannot be checked

Mandragoras: tiny servants of the devil

Medieval times: the Middle Ages

Middle Ages: the period of European history from about A.D. 500 to about 1500

Mortar: a strong deep bowl in which substances are pounded or crushed with a pestle

Mythical: existing only in the imagination

Pestle: a club-shaped tool for pounding or grinding substances in a mortar

Scrying: gazing into a mirror or crystal ball in order to learn things about future events

Supernatural: of or relating to an existence of something beyond the observable universe

Zodiac: twelve star groups or signs

INDEX

Please visit our website, www.garethstevens.com. For a free color catalog of all our high-quality books, call toll free 1-800-542-2595 or fax 1-877-542-2596.

Library of Congress Cataloging-in-Publication Data

Cox, Barbara.
Witches, wizards and dark magic / by Barbara Cox and Scott Forbes.
  p. cm. — (Creepy chronicles)
Includes index.
ISBN 978-1-4824-0267-4 (pbk.)
ISBN 978-1-4824-0268-1 (6-pack)
ISBN 978-1-4824-0269-8 (library binding)
1. Witchcraft — Juvenile literature. 2. Wizards — Juvenile literature. 3. Magic — Juvenile literature. I. Title.
BF1566.C69 2014
133.4—dc23

First Edition

Published in 2014 by
Gareth Stevens Publishing
111 East 14th Street, Suite 349
New York, NY 10003

© 2014 Red Lemon Press Limited

Produced for Gareth Stevens by Red Lemon Press Limited
Concept and Project Manager: Ariana Klepac
Designer: Emilia Toia
Design Assistant: Haylee Bruce
Picture Researcher: Ariana Klepac
Text: Scott Forbes (Forest, Castle, Desert), Barbara Cox (all other text)
Indexer: Trevor Matthews

Images: Every effort has been made to trace and contact the copyright holders prior to publication. If notified, the publisher undertakes to rectify any errors or omissions at the earliest opportunity.

Bridgeman Art Library: 2 tl and b, 3 tr, 7, 8 tl, 9 bl in box, 9 br in box, 10 bl, 11 br in box, 12 br in box, 13 tr and bl in box, 14 tr, 15 br in box, cover and 17, tr, 25 t,
Corbis: 15 tl, 23 tl in box
Getty Images: 12 bl in box, 22 tl, 24 b.
iStockphoto: other images as follows:
stick borders 8; cauldron 9; frames 9, 11; cross stitches 10, 14, 22; grunge borders 11, 15; hands 11, 13, 15; pentagram 20; ring 21;
voodoo doll 23, demon 24.
Shutterstock: all other images

KEY: t = top, b = bottom, l = left, r = right, c = center

Printed in the United States of America

CPSIA compliance information: Batch #CW14GS: For further information contact Gareth Stevens, New York, New York at 1-800-542-2595.

Gareth Stevens
Publishing